On God's River Of Time

Vivian Kearney

To Milo, my husband
and our family
who have made my life-time so lovely.

Table of Contents

Chronos for Projects, Kairos for Prayers 87

About Time

Grid

The cage where
The golden bird sings
Is time
Can it sing
Outside
As well

Song

Time
Is not totally kind
Nor too forgiving
First you kill it
Then it kills you

But O
How the song
Lingers…

On the Other Hand

Time
Is not mine
Finding His words, grace and rhyme
On this paper, for my life
Is God's sign

All You Need

After sheer existence
The space measurements
Are the first three dimensions
The fourth is time
The fifth must be love

Time's Voice

A voice calling my name
Clearly broke into my dream
Shaking me awake
It wasn't my beloved husband
It was time

Es Iz Shoyn die Hechste Zeit
– It's Already the Highest Time

On the other side
Of wrongs perceived
Absences felt as a slap
We might arrive

To lands and rivers
Of reminded friendships
Between after all relatives

And our passed parents and families
Will sigh from on high
Es iz shoyn die hechste zeit
It's high time

But we need to let
Some mourning waters pass

Co-Worker

If only
If always
Time could be
My trusted friend
Or at least
A cooperative co-worker

Time Machine
– "The Butterfly Effect"

Beware touching one particle
Of time
Stepping into
One prehistoric
Forested day
Crushing underfoot
One minute
Insect or weedy flower
Or blue butterfly

The grand kaleidoscope
Of the future
May be changed

Forever

Maybe for
The worse

Captured Clouds

The music of light
The smell of snow
The echoed smiles
Where our yesterdays
Prefigure our tomorrows

The taste of lilacs
The fabric of the day
The mansions of the winds
Places where
Captured clouds play

How much room for the unconscious
In the categorized present
How far should we sail with what charts
Into dreamy seas,
Unstructured oceans

Theme Park

Why not enjoy
The slippery slide
Of time

Knowing God has created
And is attending
The ride

And holds your hand
In the gospel-themed park
Of salvation

Tenses

Here and Now

A parallel life
In virtual time
Wouldn't have worked
As well as this one -
The best

Remember When

I don't quite recall that stage
I'm hanging on to the present
Landscape; though O Lord, keep
The album; kiss each page

Vivian Kearney

Out of the Nest

Go now my little ones
Whispered the adult oak tree
To its hundreds
Of baby acorns

That you may live and love life
After I do
What do I know
About the hard, uncaring
Cement on the driveway
Or in parking lots and streets

All I can do is form you
And help you
Let go

Floating Foundlings

"Facts are floating foundlings"
As Moses was?
How did he survive the crocodiles?

How did I
Survive the war?

How should we
Order our past, present and future
Reality river
While wondering about
Our true Seeker

Where Do We Live?

Neither the past
Nor the future
I heard
Exist

They are both subsumed
By winds
Of the present

You can or should
Only live
In the moment

But some people
Say and insist
The process
Is the only reality

And imperceptibly
Now becomes the past
As it reaches into the future

Sand trod before
Washing into
The unknown sea

Decluttering

Adorable socks for tiny feet
How can I now
Practically
Let you go?

Come On

- It's about time
Said our sweet daughter
- That you changed your cell phone

It's been ten years
You should fear
Its soon demise

Come on, catch onto
Slightly younger
Technology

- Ah, but this device
Has been so nice to me

How can I say good riddance
And good-bye

Go Ahead

It's also about time
Said our dear son
That you update
Your computer, your landline
Your answering machine
Your roof, your fence
Your window screens
Your refrigerator ….

Let us help you

Thank you, though
Will we have time enough
To get well acquainted and
On good terms
With all this
Newfangled
Nerve jangling
Stuff

Vivian Kearney

Tension of Tenses

It's no wonder
Going back perusing
Past papers, objects
Going forward, planning
Future projects
Marshalling thoughts
In line with prayers
Plus doing
Today's dailies

That housekeeping
Can be so fraught

Wrestling priorities,
Tangling with the clock

Think of It as a Dance

To the left
To the past
To the clouds
That didn't last

To the right
To the future
To the worries
About sought cures

Turn yourself and time around
With the amazing present
Open the gifts of time
That God has kindly sent

Are You Sure?

Are you
Are you sure
Are you sure you want to
Declutter, file away,
Organize possessions
Out of sight

Yet linger while
You recognize
All those molecules
Of memory

That still turn around
And bite

Point in Time

At a certain
Point in time
The memories stop waving
They have moved on
And so have you

Cat's Cradle

Cat's cradle tightening
What divine hand
Can reconfigure

That fatalistic string
Into a kind guide

That can lead us
Out of caves
Made eons ago

Made with Dad

O child that I was
O childhood that I had
Mixed with sandpaper criticism
Yet polishing acculturating
Care

Wouldn't it have been nice
To share those shaping discussions
Those unknown crafts
That secret language

Then the furniture of my life
Could be said
To have been
Made with Dad

It's Snowing

The snowflakes
Of parenting regrets
Drift down slowly
Or hurry with gusts
Of insights freezing

Blanketing past landscapes
Previously seeming
Quite verdant and lovely
Well-tended and pleasing

Now is the winter
Of our aging years
Awaiting the Son's redemption
With forgiving rays
Of understanding

Subbing in a Time Machine

Furniture from our
Beautiful valley days
Three decades ago

Seventies big square weave
Brown plaid cushions
On a heavy wooden-
Framed couch

Chairs beside
In the same construction
Clothed in small blue-white patterns
On royal blue – echoing our once
Other living room set
That hosted happy living

And again
The same dark bookshelf
That we still have
Offers free stuff for teachers
Oversized beige earphones
That used to hang from hooks
In my language classroom
On the border

Even a small yellow plastic chair
Just like ours for the kids
Dear kids
Except theirs were blue and red

I ponder
I reminisce
I wonder

Have I gone back in time
In this old-style teachers' lounge?

Beach Days

The breakers were white and foamy
Draw them
Umbrellas blue, pink, orange, green
Remember them
Wind fiercely tried
To blow pages away
Hold them
Tides called the children
Warn and watch them

Saturday vacations sounds all around
Seagulls busily nagging
Extended families picnicking

How lovely were the years
By the playful sea
In the non-valley
Rio Grande Valley

Whispering Stream

Stop
The whispering stream
Step into
The same cool river
Twice

Make each sparkling moment last

But
If you can't

Pluck the flowers of your nostalgic heart
So that they can float on beyond
Letting their rose petal perfume
Linger

To keep parts
Of your hurrying years

And hearten
Others

Back for a Day

The pictured postcard moves a little, lazily
As we drive through multiple album layers
Treading time under this forgotten wide sky
On much greener grass than before

Some places revamped, some post work continues
Memories of little feet running down a cafeteria hall
Other children play in park and library
Old home eviscerated
By disappeared trees,
Never to be restored

Montreal Visit

My aunt and I
In Montreal once
Went to a coffee pastry shop
On Queen Mary Street
Sat and talked
Enjoying the thoroughfare
Sharing the ambiance

The locusts of time
Have devoured
Many sweet pastries
Of memories

Not So Long Ago

Riding, gliding, bicycling along
Whispering streets, neat with new pavement
Shimmering in the heat, covered with
Dry leaves dancing their encouragement

A hushed together evening on a dimly lit
UTSA campus, sparkling with jeweled grass
Walking pebbled paths, past sweet smelling cedars
May such moments ever be remembered

Get Back

If we could
If we would
Go back to our beginnings

Reread and analyze
The histories of
Our own
Childhood,
Our cities,
Nations,
Religions,
Traditions

Then maybe,
Just maybe

The scales will fall
From the eyes of our hearts
And we will see and know
How to restart

A newer, calmer, freer life
Unburdened
From squabbling
Or tragic strife

Happier
With God,
Ourselves
And our neighbors

He Appeared in History

It is finished
Murmured the reviled
Rabbi, telling one of
His onlookers to look
After His mother

And the train
Of history
Took a renewed turn

On That Day

What is truth
Asked Pilate
Cynically, ostentatiously
Washing his hands
In a state-stamped
Silver bowl

But the real gold
Of Jesus' speech
Clung as dust
To his soul

Vivian Kearney

A Sixth-Century Family

A sixth century cry
Of a baby born
To doting
Celebrating parents

Is now silenced
Swallowed in deep blue space
Lost in time

Yet still echoes down
The genomes and chromosomes
Of our history-sharing minds

Once a Monument

Wind, how strong, how wild
Enough to carve the hillside
Bullying ancient villagers
With a wailing cry

Inspiring all
To get together
And lo and behold
They built an essence-strong
Stone defense
Giving us
Prehistoric monuments

To form a permanent record
Of their temporary accord

Photographs

Little did they know
They had only four more years to live
Seven with luck and stamina

Their time burned up eventually
We don't know exactly where or when
Unless they and their tattooed numbers

Were documented
As were some so carefully
By some perpetrators
Of that cleansing project

Richard III's Bones

My kingdom for a horse!
You cried
As you died
In an ancient battle

But lately
You were found buried
Under a parking lot
For modern steeds

Conquered indeed

Vivian Kearney

Blood Moon Over San Antonio

Bleeding moon veiled
By slow moving gray clouds
Like fingers of a hand
Warning us to understand

The earth is suffering more
Calamities than our usually bland
Moon, so close, speaking low
Of our precarious tomorrows

Perceptions, Choices, Advice

Coal Don't Cry

Unfair adversity
Shaping-with-pressure
Adversity

Coal don't cry
You will be shining
As diamonds
Brilliant as new stars

In our DNA
And in the dark blue sky

Roses and *Agritos*

Problematic mice in one's life
Or fierce tigers ushering you out
Ropes tying you to problems
Criticism's deafening shouts

Perceptions and paradigms
How to change the glasses
To share roses and *agritos*
With a worried one who passes

What Is It?

Are you a lace mantle
Or are you cobwebs
Are you blinged with pearls
Or are those raindrops

Are you firecrackers
Or red-bursting flowers
Nestled among
Those broad green leaves

Is the vacation sadly ending
Or is the ambivalently awaited
School year structure
Happily beginning

Wait, What Are You Saying?

This is our memorial
To the tragedy of defeat
No, it's our song of success
To our drum's righteous beat

Depends

The sky is white – no, blue – no, grey
The days go by quickly – no, slowly
The glass is half full – no, it's mostly empty
My bucket list is sad – no, actually funny

The lines rhyme methodically – no, fortuitously
The past still hurts – no, mostly it's passed by
I think I'll do nothing today – no, I'll try
To get something done beyond the sighs

What I'm reading is boring – no, it evoked a smile
What I'm writing may be silly, or again, worthwhile
Outside I'm old – inside, a difficult child
Helped by angels sent from God most versatile

Déjà Vu, Lu, Entendu

Once we traveled to Russia
Felt some of the steppe bleakness
Marveled in the cold museum
Walked a white St Petersburg night
Tiptoed around a scrutinizing hotel warden
To our room with few amenities
A wintry summer's adventuring

Later we read out loud
A travel book by a humorist
That had us in stitches
For that was just the way
It foreignly was

Still later the trip and the book
Were forgotten
Enough that
I bought it again

And – memories of memories
Echoes of echoes
Floated back, redone
In different-colored clouds

And I could hear
The ever more distant
Vacationing symphony
Of once Russia

Sometimes Fear

Sometimes fear, depression
Can feel compelled
To let go

Maybe they get tired
Of the same old shackles

Or, maybe they feel
The sun smiling
Promising a flowery,
Showery dawn

So they segue
Into intermittent worry
Dappled by
Some bright notes

Kindergarten and Post-Vacation Blues

But I went to school already
Why do I have to go again?
Let me stay home – I've got lots to do
To play with my toys, to explore
So many corners new

But I worked all last year already
Muttered my lethargic inner child
I want to wake up at all hours
And putter around the house, rearranging papers
And thought clouds, dreaming up project flowers

Seems Later

It's only six-thirty
But I got up at five-thirty
And that was eons of ideas ago

Relatively Exceptional

The cloud flashes some silver
The cool pool has some warmth
Relative to the freeze expected

Ninety-eight degrees is easier
Than one hundred

Four out of ten pain
Can be tolerated

These aging symptoms
Could be worse

This quick summer
Has stretched forever

Consider

The kitchen windows opening to
Greens and blue-pink-yellow sky
Branches delicately praying, swaying

Life beyond the here and now --
How do we see outside
Our mind's house

Looking to a land
Beyond any veiled memory

To another
Soul universe
Moving to
Numinous music

Frenemies

Do I choose independence with or from
My familiar frenemies, variegated pains?
Should I claim freedom from several
Ancient shadows, worn out sorrows?

But what baggage should I bring
Or, what will cling and not let go?
And what identity ticket to show
For what destination, on what train?

What Are the Choices?

Wandering where and wondering why
Unpleasant choices are always nigh
Time is squandered while moods are pondered
Words evaporate and smiles appear awry

New generations, north, south, east and west
Stage idealistic demands and protests
But where will those go, who knows
What hidden agendas at whose bequest

While we need less plutocracy here
Not only resources for fat cats' beer
Plans for society's cures, all our futures
Are fogged in hostilities still unclear

What choices do we make when
We only for our own good fend
Lord, lead us on Thy path right
And be our best forever Leader and Friend

It's Political

Did you or did you not
Betray us knowingly
Did you or did you not
Compromise so something
Could be salvaged
Of the dream

Will we or will we not
Go forward with more
Enlightened steps

Progressively
To alleviate many
So heavy burdens
That the 99 percent carry
And the 1 percent forget

Philosopher's Advice

Relinquish the details
The personal aches
The pains of will

To jump into universality
Where there is no slave nor free
Distinction

And all speak all languages
Intelligently and fluently
To discuss rationally

What God has made
Beautifully

Learning to Drive in San Antonio

Left lane or right lane, what will it be
On the road to work with coping technology?
Volitional, habitual, mindful, hopeful
How shall thoughts be driven by Thy call?

Right turn or left turn, exit or straight ahead
Lord help us hear Thy voice, by Thee be led
Quantitative, qualitative, how shall we live?
How many times can we be forgiven and forgive?

Conversation, recreation, mission roles and goals
What makes our time on earth a lesson for our souls?
Singing, ringing in Thy season of lights
For Thou art the *Shomer*, the guard, bright

Prayer for Our Century

Let not love end
Let not the world end
Let this hollow
Twenty-first century
Bounded by
Unfeeling technology

Be set free
From its
Heartrending mistakes
And its unworthy
Self-centered trustees

Shimmering Bridges

Butterfly bridges
Linking objects to thoughts
What is learned to what is taught
Shimmering softly
In sunbeams and moonlight

Let's leave those plaid prisons
Of self-imposed structures
Of self-criticism ever stricter
And skip on those jeweled roads
And butterfly bridges
Leading to joy

Vivian Kearney

Letting Go

Let go
And the venerable
River of culture
Will carry you
Says tradition

Let go
And you'll see
That dreaded cliff was
Just a movie
You were in before
And is now
Only virtual
Says psychology

Let go
And the prayer net
Of those who love you
Will be there

Let go
And you will be free
To walk in
Fields of mercy
To gather
Flowers of peace
To spread
Rainbows of kindness

To love
Also

Let go
And I will catch you
Says God

Outside the Kingdom of Self

Don't let
Kindness wait politely
While rudeness takes the stage
While selfishness claims
Its island castle
Imprisoning the eyes of your heart

Rather let
God's loving spirit
Open the falsely sparkling door
And ask what both of you
Can do, say, pray
To help others
To nurture nature

Driving Prayer
– Leviticus 19:18

Love your neighbor as yourself
Rejoice in the wonders of their lives
Pray for them as they drive their cars
Pondering unknown burdens,
Seeking, following
Their own North Stars

Vivian Kearney

When Should We Pray, They Asked Their Rabbi

May
Each day
Have its mission

May you
Each hour
Worship the Lord

Walk
Every minute
In His footsteps

Pray
The second before
You're taken
From this earth

You May Be on a Cruise

On the waterway of time
You may be on a cruise
With occasional piano music
Tinkling sometimes moody notes

With many stopovers
At unexpected ports
Leading to streets
That meander this way and that
To parks, monuments, restaurants, shops

Can you listen to
The inaudible voice
Follow the invisible compass
Stay connected to an intangible string

Telling you
This way, this goal
Is where, is how
Your essential soul
Wants to, needs to
Walk

Sewn Oceans

A quilted river,
A knitted sea
Life goes on
Each section a story
Every pattern belongs

Some patches rough
Some loosely sewn
Some needing repair
By the Holy Weaver
Who can redeem
Unfair cares
Unseen tears

Map, Color, Meditate

Map your world
Though it may change
By the second, by the minute
Include the new range

Color your rainbow
Though it may come and go
Note the stormy clouds
Sing hopeful songs low

Meditate if people leave you alone
Listen to the lights talking
Paint the silence blue, mauve and gold
Hide yourself in God's quiet cove

Chronos for Projects,
Kairos for Prayers

What Needed When

For us usually
Time marches in heartbeats
I wonder what is
The music of the day
Without pulsing chronos

Although is meditative kairos
A better way to glorify Thee, Lord
Or are work measurements and boundaries
Needed for service orientation

Streaming

Pray for the day's streaming hours
They're like the hurried cars
That pass you on the road
Each need protection, saving
Though oh so independent seeming

What's in Those Presents

The shape of time
Rectangular, as in this waiting room
Hilly as the gray horizon
Circular or spiral
As in repeated histories

The shades of time
White as impatience
Blue as calm
Red as worries
Green as hope

What will we do
With those awaited or unexpected
Angel-wrapped presents

Note to Self

To pause the race
To the never perfection

To return to the present's
Dissolving flowers

To write one's way
To a true identity

To read the leaves
Blowing in the wind

To interpret the clouds
In the blue, blue sky

To talk to the silence
To breathe deeply

To trace the weave
Of many an unpredictable

Wonder

Vivian Kearney

The Zen of Mistakes

Schedules advocate
You can't make mistakes
Everything must be right
The first time

Though errors' failures
Build motivations, attention
To go farther, be wiser
The next time

And keep climbing
A zen-happy mountain

Atalanta's ADD Lament, Penelope's Example

Picking up the golden apple
Losing sight of the glowing goal
You forfeited the race, despite the grace
Of the clear track for your soul

Holding on to blanketing papers
Keeping bloated realia of nostalgic memories
I pile haystacks and hide important needles
Forgetting to fulfill projects agreed

Let me stop unweaving the tapestry of time
Given by the Father of connections and rhyme
Who still leads me on roads not yet taken
Who always patiently offers redemption

Today's Idea

I was
So certain
I could keep
That wisp of an idea
A promising insight
Leading to who knows
How many more

But it flew away
Or was it buried
Beneath the sand castles
That the inexorable
Ocean of the day
Washed clear away

How You See It Generically

The day as a melody
First unidentified

The day as a brook
Its journey unknown

The day as a flower
Dancing with
An imagined rainbow

The day as a tree
Not waiting to pray

Vivian Kearney

A Certain Saturday

Driving early we spy
Star-shaped lilies
That bloom just for a summer day
Christmas-lit fire truck setting out
To check if everyone's okay
On this gray and stormy morning
Not without danger warnings
Though here we are in church anyways
To practice singing for a hopefully
Sunny Sunday

It's Your Future

 - But I don't want to play piano
So I don't want to practice
 - You don't know what you'll love later
Or what skills you'll wish you could know

 - But I want to play games
All day long when I can
 - But these won't help you over the years
Please let preparation hold your hand
As you move into future lands

Day Break

Dawn's light
Through white window blinds -
My gentle alarm

Morning Rapping Revisited

Just another workday morning
You already had your warning
If you don't soon get out of bed
Panic will run manic in your head
Now go, now go
Don't be so slow
Your teenagers awake
They must not be too late
For the bath run the water
Don't let it get any hotter
Now iron necessary clothes
Should it be these or should it be those
Find your better shoes
Why do you always lose the clues
As to where they hide
Minutes as unstoppable as the tide
Now for the hose
All of this shows
Should have gotten ready
Long ago and kept all steady
And on schedule
Within the rules
Of our respective schools
Now where is the brush
Doesn't it know we're in a rush
Now for a ribbon and some pins
Lord, forgive me for my sins
Of leaving this to the last hour

Perhaps it's yet within your power
To help us arrive there on time
And still enjoy a day quite fine
Then open the garage, get into the car
Without it we won't get very far
Then run around the house and scurry
Checking all so wouldn't worry
About electricity or doors unlocked
Examine at last the pursuing clock
Can't believe it, all seems done
Thanks to You Lord, Holy Spirit and Son
When it's seconds that we need
Time obeys as Your trained steed
For You are Master of the minutes, tide and wind
World and universe indeed

Linear or ADD or Scanner

Our regular jobs demand that we be linear
From dawn to dusk, not letting rust
Or flowers grow on the day's train tracks

Might ADD or scanning be a more painterly thing
With layers of colors jostling for attention
Maybe it's another way
To appreciate our Artist-King

Past, Now and Beyond

Role-play to get a little more linear
When I give you this part of the string
You can run with what's next
Practice; know where it leads
Then you won't feel the need
To drop it so much, to forget it
And run out in left field

Look how God gave us mathematical
Formulas, patterns, algorithms, games
So measured, so quantitative

To work with, to enjoy, for employment
In this, His interactive, interconnected
Gift of a world
You will be happy now and later
That you did

Too Cute

Redbird, redbird
Perched on our fence
Do you know how pretty you are
Too beautiful
For our busy schedule

Martha and Mary
– Luke 10: 38-42

Martha and Mary
By-words, sigh-words
Martha living in the work-world
Present all around
By chores bound

Mary listening to Jesus
Unfazedly, amazedly

What if Martha took a little
Of Mary's interests and was blessed

But to be fair and square
Mary would also have to help a little
With the preparations

Enabling her sister
To take a spiritual vacation

As should we
Joyfully

To The Family Dressmakers

First you stitch
Then you embroider
Then you plaid
The threads of your life
Then you quilt
All those beautiful memories
Diligently stitching
Every capable minute

Always sewing, always hoping
For good projects
And outcomes
For your beloved ones,

Thank you. Thank God for you
Freda, Mania, Pepka, Jacques

Encouragement

Heart-shaped shadows inside
Of outside branches
Blowing, dancing
Delightfully dappling
The white blinds
This sunny, cold morning

How can I not marvel,
Meditate, contemplate,
And be exceedingly
Grateful

Retirement

Day's problem solved
Of what to do first
Although with procrastination's
Lumpy fare
I played games
With time's critical stare

Now the day is almost gone
And more chores
And projects left undone
How to regain the lost hours and minutes
And steward the next day
In another spirit

The Moody

The melancholy, moody
Mid-afternoon hours
Yawn critically

Still too far from
The forgiving relief
Day-is-doneness
Of the evening

When projects can't be finished
Anyways

And night flies in
On moon-colored
Butterfly wings

Free Time

When a day moves away
From its usual metabolism
It becomes a foreign country
To meander with mood tourism

Maybe to review
Its fascinating topography
With a documentary
Memory video later

Vivian Kearney

Pale Ice Cream Scoop Sun

Such strangely downward flowing leaves
On yonder unnamed tree
Under a pale ice-cream scoop sun
Shedding an uncertain light
Over this mysterious afternoon

Everything humming obscure runes
In a vaguely transcendental mood

Seasons

The school year has just finished
Now I'm time's child
And it's mine to manage

To steer through
The blue, white, yellow, green rooms
The purple, blue, green, orange plans

That await the hide and surprise
Adventures of
The just beginning summer

………………..

Summer's almost gone
Working fall is coming on
I've been turning around
This old house too long

Grumpy mood masking
Deep thanksgiving
Some projects finished
Some illnesses healing

Bless the past and present, o my soul
It has been a season of gold
God is tying up many knots
Even of futures yet untold

Four Caretakers

God sends
An angel of a morning
With pink and blue wings
The twin of yesterday's twilight

Shaking me out of dreams
That want to sit around the campfire
Of previous events
Nostalgic tunes
Lovely kairos time

Chronos, a rather strict caretaker
Stirs the pensive embers
Saying, I was also sent by our Lord
To be your fourth caretaker
To spell out your mission
For the day

So
Now
Go

Poetry Can Stop Time

Smile, you're on candid simile
A passing fancy
That stops time

What's Good About Waiting

Wait - Give Me Some Time

Let the bright light of dawn
Shine this sleepy morning
Let the pale pink-white wall
With its popcorn texture
Be contemplated
And described

Let the silence
Play its music
Let Plato's ideal forms
Float above the material world
Let chronos wait for kairos
Just a little longer

Resting by the Side of I-10

While we're resting by the side of I-10

Will there be drama in the painted landscape
Will the clouds move into new configurations
Will some birds populate the scraggly branches
Will the furry grasses wave expectantly

Waiting for our eyes to caress them lovingly
Waiting for our wheeled house to resume rolling
Waiting for us to rejoin the zooming highway
Waiting for the rest of this trip
To our previous home

Christ the Psychologist

If you can understand
The patterns of
The beam in your eye
The tears in your thoughts
The sighs of your soul

Then maybe
You can discuss it with Christ
And He'll say

I was waiting for you to realize
And to be made whole

At the Hospital

Chance, the aqua green curtain
Topped by white netting
The machines waiting to measure

Or is it planned, all planned
To give our freely-acting God
The chance to heal us
To bring salvation

....

Moments on the other side of nervousness
Ride by slowly on the bicycle of the empty morning

So calm does have something to do with happenstance
And present's questions are quieted
By some good news tests

....

Gurgling machine in the waiting
Hospital room while minutes tick
To yet another date with a procedure
While we get to the hours inured

Vivian Kearney

Brick the walls here,
Stone blocks on the opposite building
Green the leaves teaching patience, clouds saying
Why don't you meditate during this gracious
Gift of time while you wait

. . . .

The twinkling seas of city lights
The solemn processional of cars
The mauve waters of evening settling in
The oceans of hills ringing the horizon

The sun writes his last colorful farewells
To this panorama from the hospital window
Waiting for tomorrow's positive dismissal
After this hospital trip's wake-up call

While We Wait

Let's write a poem about waiting
Nervously in an airport amidst
Detached bustling travelers

In an office, counting
Bricks and windows

In a dentist's reception room
Diving into the wallpaper landscape of
Prowling tigers on exotic islands

On a bench in a gym
Of busy self-improvement

Imagining a parallel
Universe of job possibilities

Wondering what will be
Next year's reality

Ask Them

Elephants in the room
Biding their time, waiting
Until someone would and could
Let them out of their cages
Of secrets

Ask them
Listen to their sage
Gray advice and recollections
Because, as you know,
Elephants never forget

Dispensational Revelation

Dispensational the saving way
God wants to show each the truth
And the light
Of His loving message
Patiently He awaits people
Of all persuasions

Heaven doesn't close
At a certain earthly hour
Only God knows the souls
Only He can each cover

For He is Jesus Who is love
Yearning for everyone to be saved
Thankfully we cannot judge
But we can walk the given road
Of charity and grace

He Is Here

Waiting for the thought
To become music
For objects to be infused
By dancing light
For nerves
That say we can't

To hear
That God can
He is here

Why Am I So Nervous?

God just gave me
Time enough
To write
To rewrite
To print
To reprint

And enough ink besides

Meditative Waiting

Why don't we
Measure the minutes
By the grass growing
Or wilting in the heat

Why don't we
Ride the waves of hours
Changing the surfboard often

Why don't we
Listen to the day passing
Mark it with alphabet adjectives
Describing our Alpha and Omega
Everlasting Abba

Ages That Wait

Baby-
Hood
Unable
If unhelped
To move much
From one place
To another

Old age
Again losing
Powers of locomotion
Traveling in
Smaller and smaller
Circles

But both
Are beautiful

Waiting to be
Picked up

At The End of the Day

Vivian Kearney

New Stage

Where will we go, what will we do
When we forget what to renew

In the shatterlands of a new stage
Pondering the shutters of another age

This Far

You have come this far
With pains, anxieties, joys
Clouds and jeweled rays
At every age

Stepping up in a spiral staircase
Or a ladder like the one Jacob saw
To the mentoring, ancestral
Angel stars

Who open the door
To heaven's agelessness

Vivian Kearney

Carpe Diem as We Sail

We are all sailing on lesser or better
Vessels towards the end of the world
The drop-off is real, though some cruise ships
Would have us forget that certain cliff

Can we control the current, exercising
Power over the wind and waves
Or is there a ladder from the clouds to climb
Out of the ocean into eternity's light

Let's seize the day, the chance to pray
For fellow passengers on every ship
And hope for a good port and a way
Where all can be forever saved

Documentary of a Quest

The amazing
Seventy-year old man
Tried but failed
To complete with his team
The wondrous expedition
To the end of a continent
And cried

He was comforted by
His younger team-mates
Then they all found
Many more happy views
By going
Another way

Can I rely on
My weakening
Thoughts, memories
Muscles, words
To take me
In varied ways

To more moments
Views and insights
Of truth and beauty

And will they
Lead to God
Or ever recede

Until…

Souvenir in My Wardrobe

She knitted, she sent
A lovely, off-white, textured,
Woolen sweater

For cold Canadian winters
To keep herself and
Her family warm
For good survivor lives

Not quite the right
Covering
For San Antonio

But a dear
Posthumous, put away
Souvenir

Vivian Kearney

Things Change

You
Can't step into
The same river
The same language
The same house
Twice

Drops and phonemes
And molecules
Keep flowing, changing

Unfortunately
My body size and health
Do too

Little Green Parrot

Where is my memory
That little green parrot?

It flew up to distracting trees
Camouflaging itself among the leaves

Singing some barely audible notes

When it lived in
My younger brain's golden cage

Its cries were so clear

Hide and Seek

Time, like a merry child
Plays hide and seek
Every once in a while

Then peeks out
From silent corners
And shouts –
You're it

You're the person with all the ailments now
Who can't walk so fast, who can't sleep well
Nor digest whatever, whenever

Mostly that scamp hands over
Melancholy messages
About numbered hair
And numbered steps

Keep Calm

When
More of my hair
Falls out
What will I do
With those
Mirror blues

I'll find extensions
And wigs and try
To keep calm
And carry on

Don't Feel Guilty

The river of time
Moves faster and faster

So don't feel guilty, o soul
If leaves and flowers
Lights and shadows
Of words and thoughts
Move so quickly

They're planning to build
More ships and shelters

Hiding

Hushed and hiding
The corners of my mind

What are those brain cells
And synapses going through
So heavy and blue

Strangers to myself
And others

As senior moments
Accumulate
Invading

Clever bucket list plans
That only Jesus
Can appreciate
And revive

Application

Skill set
You bet
Let me try
To show you why

I'm still good
Knock on wood
For this work

Just give me the word

Retirement Planet

Okay, so we are travelers
Who once landed in work's spaceship
But now it's gone and left us stranded
On this retirement planet
No way either for short term trips

Let us love where we are
The closer flowers, the distant stars
Our mission is to help and pray
For all near and far away

Vivian Kearney

Once Upon a Time

Once upon a time
I had some time

To surf the present
To dream new dawns
To draw open doors

Now what are the days
Good for

To contemplate
God's timeless hand

Guiding, interpreting me
With loving understanding

Revisiting

I'm rereading childhood books
Singing those early songs
Rewatching old movies
When the days are too long

I bought a wood and metal washboard
Not seen since ages ago
Maybe I'll relearn my first language
And try to knit again and sew

The circle is trying to close itself
Or maybe God makes it more of a spiral
Echoing upwards out of my childhood
Leading to new gardens spiritual

Tell My Cells

Tell my cells
How long I have left
Will the chariot be sweet
And swift
Or long time arriving

May the eves of our years
Be peaceful and comforted

May the autumn
Of all lives be lovely

If country, age, culture, world
Say otherwise

They aren't wise
(Or kind)

Not Eden

Every person's every cell
Can imagine in its own language
Wondrous landscapes, healing fruit trees
Wafting flowers, paradise walks

And knows very well
What is not Eden

However

However, all is not
Totally scientifically
Predestined

Creative decisions
In the morning, day and evening
Lift our thought neurons
Way above biology

Aging Adjectives

Garrilous, crotchety, crabby, spry
We're asking grumpily why
People give us these adjectives
And think we're old

While inside
The teen soul
Still dances

Generational

But I'm your age
Just for a longer time

Perspectives may be different
Perceptions are often the same

And I love to laugh also
To discuss events, people

Only don't move me aside
Into a generational
Scary Jurassic Park

Passing

Vivian Kearney

Hold Us Together

Hold us together, I said
To the videotapes of biographies
I was transcribing
To let us keep
Family histories

But I hadn't remembered
Or counted on
Their strength of character
These relatives
Aren't just past actors

Their ghosts in the machine
Pulled me into their stories
Claiming for me
Inspiring for us
Their survivor qualities

Persuading, promising
That their souls live on
Outside time and space

Though their worldly seasons
Under the earthly sun
Have come and gone

Gabriel García Márquez

A yellow rose for García Márquez
So he could look into its labyrinth
Every day and retrace the petalled path
Back to Colombia's magic butterflies

What could, what should help me
Retrace mine

For me a coral rose bush
The one sometimes growing
Outside our front window

To predict our dances together
Into the smiling sunset

Daily Prayer

Love at first sight
Love of my life
I saw you standing there
At registration
In your black corduroy jacket

Moving a little to the left
Then right into our Latin class

Let us forever
Stay together
Happily talking
To our matchmaking Father

Anne Frank's Journal

My dearest Anne
Don't worry, don't fear
You haven't disappeared

Though
Tragically stopped
When you were led away

Your diary
Detailing suffering
In hiding
Has made you
A forever journalist

You are brought
To virtual life
Every time
Your story, our history
Is read, told

Your soul continues
To walk
On our roads

Another Friend's Passing

Where are you little red flowers?
Dormant as the sleeping bumble bees
But the leaves and roots will continue
To absorb the rain, sun and sky

Where are you years, relatives, friends gone by
Gone with yesterday's refreshing snows
But the kind soul, talk, deeds will continue
To affect family, friends, neighbors

Message from
Federico García Lorca

Though I am and was
Led away
To my death

My soul from beyond
Can tell you
About my last minutes on earth
With my poems

My frightened, praying
About-to-be ripped heart

Taking as souvenirs
The fateful, tolling bells
Flowers, lilies and bees
Of my home
Nearby

As well as
My childhood's feathered cap

And I still also have
And know how to use

That dragon-slaying sword
My reverberating words

Vivian Kearney

When I'm Gone

When I'm gone
Objects, speak for me

My miniscule chain clasp
That attached important wallets
To any chosen purse

Tablecloths and books
Drawers cluttered
Bags packed
House filled

With sweet nothings
And much used stuff

Before you too
Are swept away
Wept away

And perhaps recycled

Light Show

See the stars
On their twinkle toes
Waltzing all over the heavens
Humming in the dimmed sky
Ballroom with its lights
Long gone by

Loved ones, relatives, friends, mentors, neighbors
Is it you?

Enjoying untiring
Spirit dancing

Vivian Kearney

Corner of Fredericksburg Road and Huebner

The cemetery protects
Those old growth trees
As does USAA
On the other side

Where have all the others gone
That shaded the hills there too

Back to the graveyards
Of concrete and cement

Let's remember to
Commemorate them
Also

Argument

What can you, what should you fight
At the dying of the light
That fed you, led you so brightly
In your meaning-seeking life

Can you, should you rage
Cursing all still around
Rather bless the witnesses, wave gently
As on the last trip you're bound

Talking to Mallarmé

Tears on the lake of time
Without love from on high
Can freeze in the coldness
Of an uncaring sky

But the new creature, the swan
Is freed by the Son
His warming embrace,
His loving arms

Time – Our Frenemy;
God – Our Hope

Surviving Life's Race

Time will run
Once it danced
Or sang
Went on
Pilgrimage

But eventually
Time will run
Out

Yet God will
Still stay with us
Will help us
Survive life's race
With grace

Lullaby

I am the pillow
Soft and warm
Caressing and soothing
In any storm

I am the trees
Tall and spiritual
Dusting your skies
I am the trees

I am the flower
Tiny, colorful power
To disseminate
Loveliness, happiness
I am the flower

I am the rock
Stalwart and sure
Dependable, unbendable
I am the rock

I am the bird
Mighty in flight
Bringing the word
To the earth so fair
I am the bird

I am the Lamb
Perfect and pure
A sacrificial cure
For all your sins
I am the Lamb

I am the rainbow
Letting you know
There is hope
You can cope
With all rains
I am the rainbow

I am your pillow
Lay down your head
I will hold you, enfold you
I am the loving Lord true

He's Real

I dreamed that we
Ran out into the woods
Where we saw a great light
Beauty, goodness, truth
Radiated from His words bright

I woke up and in the sky, behold
His shining momento of gold
The Son smiled – it's a new day
And I am with you always